AMERICAN CITIES

# SAN ANTONIO

Lily Erlic

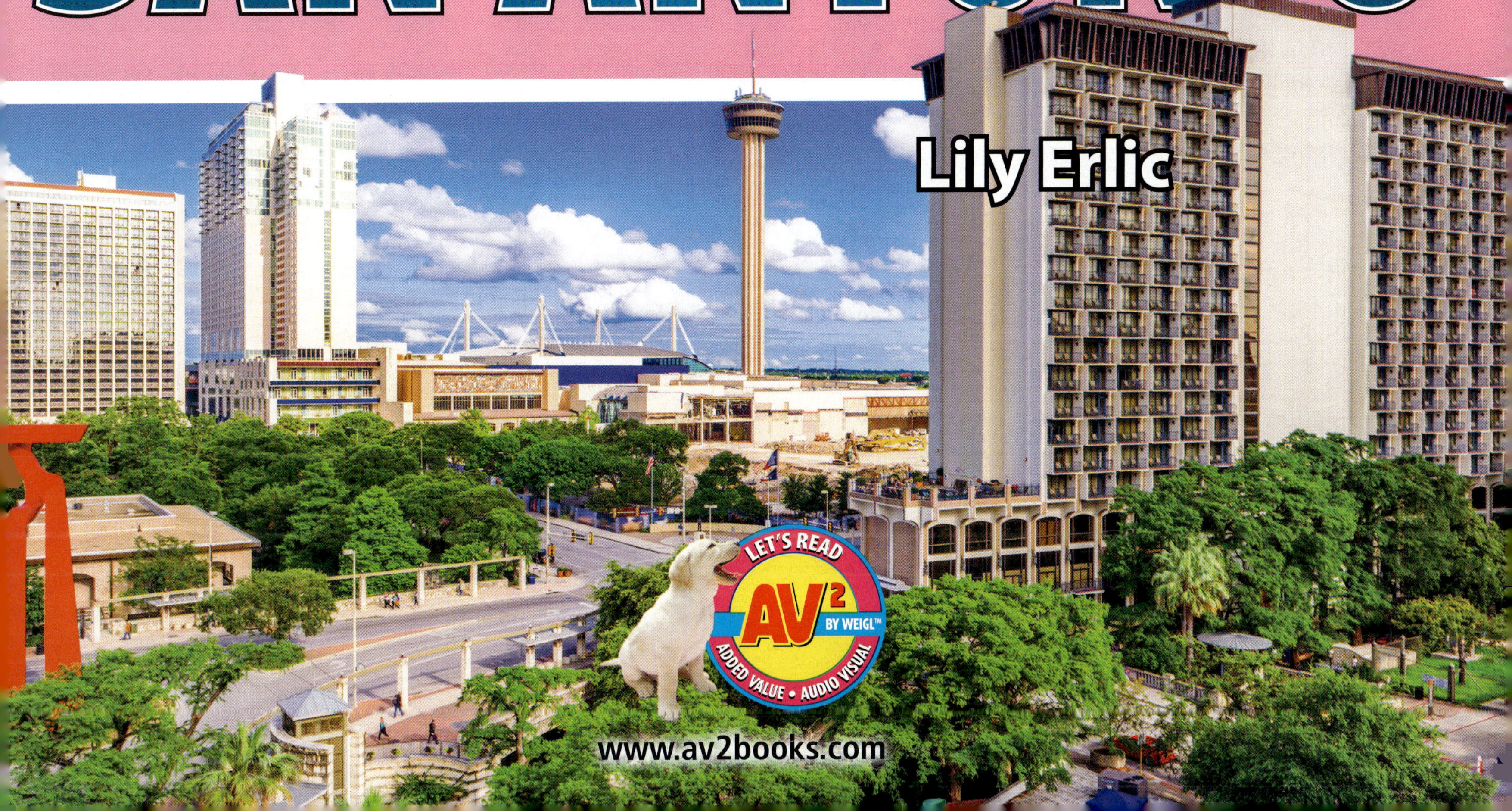

LET'S READ AV2 BY WEIGL
ADDED VALUE • AUDIO VISUAL

www.av2books.com

Published by AV$^2$ by Weigl
350 5$^{th}$ Avenue, 59$^{th}$ Floor New York, NY 10118
Website: www.av2books.com



Library of Congress Cataloging-in-Publication Data

Names: Erlic, Lily, author.
Title: San Antonio / Lily Erlic.
Description: New York, NY : AV2 by Weigl, [2018] | Series: American cities | Audience: Grades K-3.
Identifiers: LCCN 2018048673 (print) | LCCN 2018049046 (ebook) | ISBN 9781489694713 (Multi User ebook) | ISBN 9781489694775 (Single User ebook) | ISBN 9781489694690 (hardcover : alk. paper) | ISBN 9781489694706 (softcover)
Subjects: LCSH: San Antonio (Tex.)--Juvenile literature.
Classification: LCC F394.S2114 (ebook) | LCC F394.S2114 E76 2018 (print) | DDC 976.4/351--dc23
LC record available at https://lccn.loc.gov/2018048673

Printed in the United States of America in Brainerd, Minnesota
1 2 3 4 5 6 7 8 9 0 22 21 20 19 18

112018
051118

Project Coordinator: Heather Kissock Designer: Ana María Vidal

Weigl acknowledges Getty Images, Alamy, Shutterstock, and iStock as the primary image suppliers for this title.

# Contents

# Get to Know San Antonio

San Antonio is the second largest city in the state of Texas. The city was built around the San Antonio River. Today, the River Walk is a popular place to visit. This area in the city's downtown is full of shops and things to see.

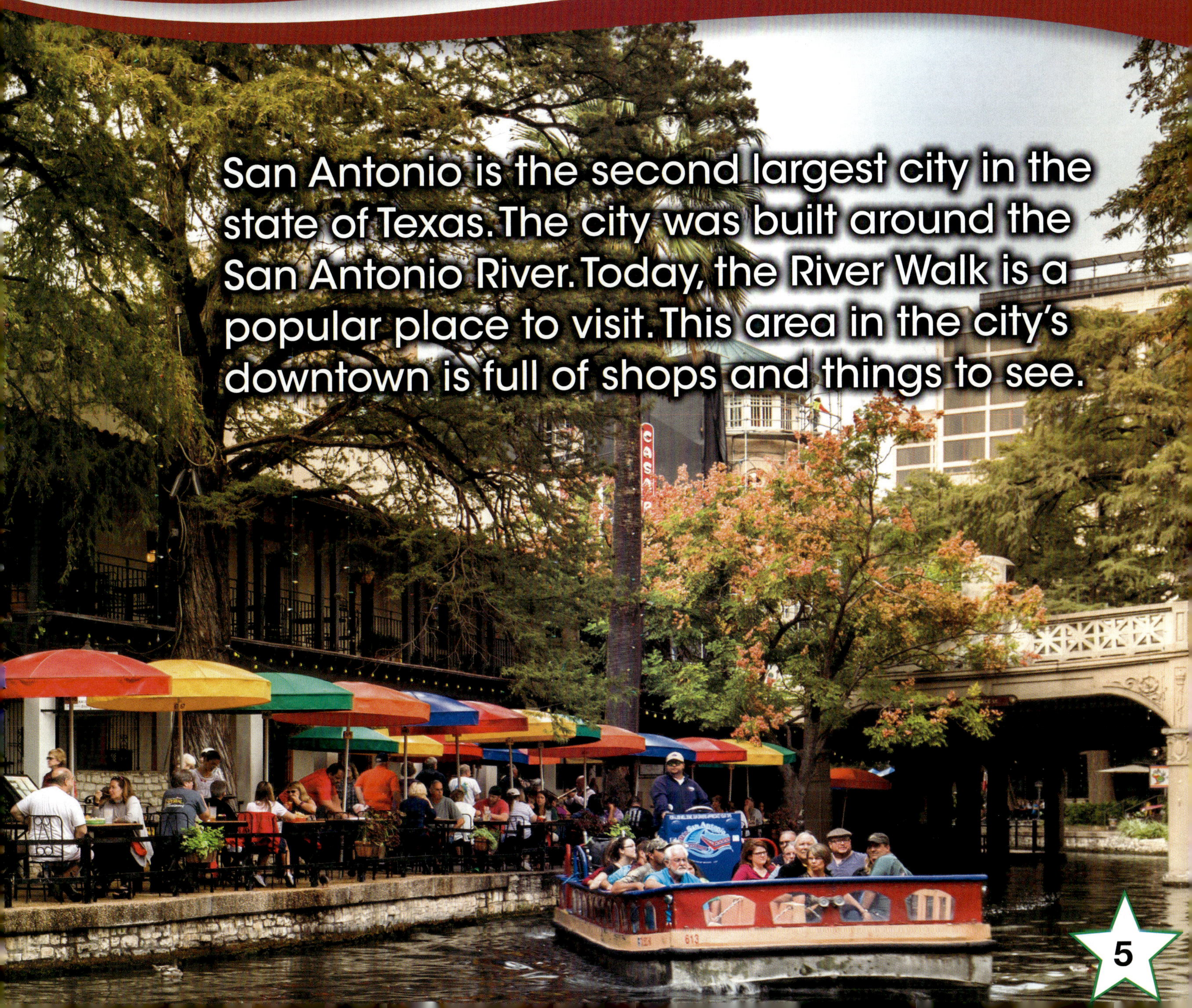

Map of Texas
United States Map
Alaska
Hawai'i
Texas
OKLAHOMA
NEW MEXICO
ARKANSAS
TEXAS
LOUISIANA
Fort Worth Stockyards, Fort Worth
AUSTIN
Space Center Houston, Houston
SAN ANTONIO
Big Bend National Park
MAP LEGEND
San Antonio
Capital City
Texas
United States
Mexico
Water
SCALE
0
60 Miles
N
Texas Seaport Museum, Galveston
MEXICO
Gulf of Mexico

# Where Is San Antonio?

San Antonio is in the south part of Texas. It is 80 miles southwest of Austin, the state's capital city. You can get there from San Antonio by taking the I-10 and I-35 highways.

There are other places to visit in Texas. You can plan a trip using a road map. Which roads could you take from San Antonio to get to these other places? How long might it take you to get to each place?

| TRAVELING TEXAS |
| --- |
| San Antonio to Fort Worth 268 miles |
| San Antonio to Houston 197 miles |
| San Antonio to Big Bend National Park 409 miles |
| San Antonio to Galveston 248 miles |

# Climate

Summers in San Antonio are hot and humid. Temperatures can climb to more than 90 degrees Fahrenheit. The city has about 220 sunny days every year.

San Antonio has mild winters. The city rarely gets snow. Rain falls mostly in the spring and fall.

San Antonio gets an average of **0 inches** of **snow** every year.

Face

# Population and Geography

San Antonio is the seventh largest city in the United States. More than 1.5 million people live there. It is one of the fastest growing cities in the country.

San Antonio was built on top of the Edwards Aquifer. This is a body of water found deep under the ground. The city gets much of its water from this aquifer.

# Many Peoples

Native Americans were the first people to live in the San Antonio area. Spanish settlers arrived in the 1700s. In 1718, Father Antonio de Olivares built a mission in the area. He wanted to help the people who lived there. This mission became known as the Alamo.

Over the years, four more missions were built. More people came to live in the area. The settlement grew to become the city of San Antonio.

San Antonio was the **capital** of **Texas** from **1772** until **1824**.

ANTON

# Tourism

The Alamo is one of San Antonio's top tourist sites. A well-known battle was fought there in 1836. Today, people visit the Alamo to learn more about the battle and the people who fought in it.

Every year, San Antonio holds its Stock Show & Rodeo. More than 2 million people attend the show. Many come to watch cowboys ride bulls and wrestle steers.

The **Battle of the Alamo** lasted for **13 days.**

# Sports

San Antonio is home to four major sports teams. The Spurs are the city's basketball team. The Missions play baseball for the city. The Rampage play hockey.

San Antonio has a soccer team, too. The San Antonio FC plays at Toyota Field.

19
TISSOT
Frost
SPURS
10

U.S. AIR FORCE
567
737 TRG
321 TRS
737 TRG
321 TRS

# Economy

Many people who live in San Antonio work for the military. The city is home to four different military locations. Together, they bring more than $15 billion to the city every year.

Tourism also makes money for the city. More than 34 million people visit San Antonio each year. They spend money at the city's stores and restaurants.

**1 out of 8**
San Antonians works in the **tourism** industry.

# San Antonio Timeline

**15,000 years ago**
Native Americans live on the land now known as San Antonio.

**1718**
Father Antonio de Olivares founds the area's first mission.

**1821**
San Antonio becomes part of the Mexican Empire.

**1836**
Texans fight for independence from Mexico at the Battle of the Alamo.

**1845**
San Antonio becomes part of the new U.S. state of Texas.

**1939**
Construction of the River Walk begins.

**1968**
The Tower of the Americas opens.

**2018**
San Antonio celebrates its 300th birthday.

# Things to Do in San Antonio

**Main Plaza**
Built in the 1700s, the Main Plaza is the historic heart of San Antonio. Festivals and other events are held here throughout the year.

**Tower of the Americas**
Visitors get great views of the city from the top of this 750-foot-tall tower.

## San Antonio Zoo

More than 9,000 animals are found at the San Antonio Zoo. One way to see them is by taking a ride on the zoo's miniature train.

## Natural Bridge Caverns

Located just outside the city, these are some of the largest caverns in the United States. Visitors walk under a 60-foot-long limestone bridge to enter the caverns.

## Kiddie Park

This is the oldest children's amusement park in the country. Visitors can go on pony rides or play carnival games. They can also ride on a carousel made in 1918.

# KEY WORDS

Research has shown that as much as 65 percent of all written material published in English is made up of 300 words. These 300 words cannot be taught using pictures or learned by sounding them out. They must be recognized by sight. This book contains 101 common sight words to help young readers improve their reading fluency and comprehension. This book also teaches young readers several important content words, such as proper nouns. These words are paired with pictures to aid in learning and improve understanding.

| Page | Sight Words First Appearance |
|---|---|
| 4 | get, know, to |
| 5 | a, and, around, city, in, is, of, place, river, second, see, state, the, things, this, walk, was |
| 7 | are, by, can, could, each, from, how, it, long, might, miles, other, part, take, there, these, where, which, you |
| 8 | about, an, days, every, has, more, than, year |
| 11 | country, found, its, live, much, on, one, people, under, water |
| 12 | as, came, first, four, he, help, many, over, until, were, who |
| 15 | come, for, learn, watch, well |
| 16 | at, home, play, too |
| 19 | also, different, makes, out, they, together, work |
| 20 | land, now |
| 21 | begins, new, opens |
| 22 | do, great, here |
| 23 | animals, children, go, just, made, or, some, them, way |

| Page | Content Words First Appearance |
|---|---|
| 4 | San Antonio |
| 5 | area, downtown, River Walk, shops, Texas |
| 7 | Austin, highways, road map, trip |
| 8 | average, climate, fall, inches, rain, snow, spring, summers, temperatures, winters |
| 11 | body, Edwards Aquifer, geography, ground, population, United States |
| 12 | Alamo, capital, Father Antonio de Olivares, mission, Native Americans, settlement, settlers |
| 15 | battle, bulls, cowboys, sites, steers, Stock Show & Rodeo, tourism |
| 16 | baseball, hockey, Missions, Rampage, sports, Spurs, teams, Toyota Field |
| 19 | economy, industry, locations, military, money, restaurants, stores |
| 20 | independence, Mexican Empire, Mexico, Texans, timeline |
| 21 | birthday, construction, Tower of the Americas |
| 22 | events, festivals, heart, Main Plaza, views, visitors |
| 23 | carousel, games, Kiddie Park, Natural Bridge Caverns, park, ride, San Antonio Zoo, train |